The Rose
of January

Geoffrey Nutter

The Rose of January

Wave Books   Seattle and New York

Published by Wave Books www.wavepoetry.com

Wave Books titles are distributed to the trade by
Consortium Book Sales and Distribution
Phone: 800-283-3572 / SAN 631-760X

This title is available in limited edition hardcover
directly from the publisher

Library of Congress Cataloging-in-Publication Data
Nutter, Geoffrey, 1968–
The rose of January / Geoffrey Nutter. — 1st ed.
p. cm.
ISBN 978-1-933517-69-8 (alk. paper)
I. Title.
PS3614.U88R67 2012
811'.6—dc23
2012028571

Printed in the United States of America

9 8 7 6 5 4 3 2 1 First Edition

Wave Books 035

The author would like to acknowledge and thank the editors
of the journals in which some of these poems first appeared:
Mark Bibbins at The Awl, Molly Lou Freeman at Carnet de route,
Rebecca Wolff at Fence, Nate Pritts at H_NGM_N, Rae Winkelstein
at The Iowa Review, Michael Morse and Minna Proctor at The Literary
Review, Joel Craig at Make, Micah Bateman at Petri Press, Danny
Lawless at Plume, Colin Cheney and R. A. Villanueva at Tongue:
A Journal of Writing & Art, and Travis Smith at Yalobusha Review.

}

Lettuce, apple, or melon, in season—so long as it is good.... When their hour is past do not try to move the hand back on the dial & do them again but try that undone something which is in season now, celery, ice, or cucumbers.   —Ralph Waldo Emerson

Metalmark

Last night I dreamed
a giant butterfly,
its enormous wings striped
with myriad colors,
was drifting silently
over the green hills
and above the bridges
and the towers of the city.
It was not akin
to a flowered matrix
of calculated vernal
arrangements, nor the yellow
undulation of a wave
seen by a child at eventide.
It was as if great marble
blocks and grinding stones
came ambling from the water mills
to watch the human pageant,
and there instead were met
with the essence of that pageant's

leave-taking. And I for one
wanted to ascend the winding
Chinese staircase to draw
nearer to its medium
and there behold it. But
that I beheld it from the sky
was what the dream made
not probable, but possible.

Colossus

Ships were sailing through the narrow passage
straddled by the legs of the colossus.
The silver-violet clouds drifted past its shoulders.
The head of the colossus lay in a tangled mass of sedge
on shore near where the ships were docking.
And someone, perhaps a sailor, had placed a ladder
up against the tilted head of the colossus.
The fallen arm of the colossus,
upright in the silt of the shallow bay,
rose from the water; its outstretched fingers
glittered in the sun. A tower on the shore
looked as old and ruined
as a boot in which a hundred orphans live.
The children swarmed from the tower.
They climbed through the mouth
into the head of the colossus.

Samuel Pepys

I was reading Samuel Pepys's diary
on the train, and as I read I noticed
something: that I was sleeping
when he was sleeping, and waking
when he woke. And then too I found
that I was garbed in richest
suit of pearl, like Samuel Pepys,
and furthermore I found that when
Samuel Pepys lay beside his wife
abed till late into the morning
I too lay beside my espoused.
With tailors at work on the quarter-deck
cutting yellow cloth into the fashion
of a crown, he is dining on a lobster,
on dozens of little oysters, and on
partridges and sparrows, and marrow
bones in a dish, a dish of prawns
and cheese, a loin of veal, two dozen

larks, anchovies and a neat's tongue . . .
and so am I. He sends for a cup of tea,
he hears a sermon, gets news of traitors
being quartered; you have rued
sly with wonder and dejection these daily
entries. While he is being garbed in his suit
of lavender and pearl, like some beautiful
creature of the sea, the berry-sized samples
of a man's small life are ripening:
presents, rich fur, carpets, cloths of tissue,
and sea-horse teeth, perforce what makes up day.
Divide it from its essence like a tissue
of sparks above the black plums of fire.
You must echo your sad, real experiences
somehow, shards of a large glass globe
in the brown and fallen leaves. Samuel Pepys,
I know that, someday soon, you will read
the story of my life, as I read yours,
immersed in details. Monuments will rise then
from amaranth and stand again, be reinhabited
by phantoms, the fragrant spired leaves
that are touched and touched again
later by the same hand.

Here Is a Clock Tower

Whoever wishes to build a clock tower
should study this one that I once saw.
The first story is square, with four small gables.
The second has eight panels and a roof,
and above that four smaller gables with
a broad space between each. And there
are foliated heads of bearded men in stone,
and ornamental leaves, an apple-colored
glaze fired on. Behind the clock tower
the bright tint of distant, well-wooded mountains.
Beyond the mountains, the palatial clouds,
the clouds of pearl and rose, and then the sea
plain as octagon jade . . . plain as distance.
There is another clock tower, that tells
a different time, under the clouds of dusk.
Now, it is both another and the same day,
fleeting, small, refreshing as a raindrop.
Now it seems you're standing in its shadow.

And now, again, you come up against
the limits of a moment, with a searing
intuition of its zenith. A robin
pulls a worm up from between the blades
of wet grass near the fallen obelisk.
In the interior of the tribunes of the nave,
looking toward the last bay, the notary
public watches merchants bring back
Syrian glass for envoys in the rain.
The foliate heads of stone that stare
ornately through the leaves, are now
all talking amongst themselves, Sir,
but not to you.

The Circle

Are you going to see the circle?
Some say it is a ring, some a circle, some a chain of rings,
 some a chain.
It will be rising over the park at nightfall.
It will rise, burning, and form a burning circle in the sky.
It will be a very precious hour.
The whole city will turn out, in the grass, in trees, on rooftops.
The very rich will watch from dragon boats along the waterfront.

Oh yes, it's winter, the rail tops are frozen, blue, and the sun is
 nothing.
Tremendous flakes are drifting down from the mountains.
The sun is nothing. The sky is nothing.
The sun is going down behind the dark, motionless peaks.
People are coming out of the buildings like lovers.
Now we are watching ourselves from above.
We are watching ourselves from the buildings, then from the
 mountaintops, and from the sky.
Look: we're watching ourselves from the sun.

We're beautiful walking on the earth, under stars, under clouds,
   under buildings, under trees, hand in hand.
We can be what we were meant to be, and have known we always
   were, thrilled and redesigned like tigers by our lovers.
We are everywhere, instantly; the electric stations crackle on full
   power, running on the ghost impulses of the waterfalls.
The million city lights flicker for an instant like sunlight passing
   over canebrake, they crash off and plunge us into night's sweet
   grape leaves.
The night is cavernous and gorgeous, endless, carnivorous.
Great pads of snow are forming in silence, ice forms in radiant
   darkness.
Owls and boulders and gargoyles count down slowly from one
   thousand in a whisper.

And the circle is rising, as promised.
It is a ring, a chain, a V, a sphere, a burning sign.
It's burning off the snow and firing the rails.
It's rising over the buildings, over trees.
If it happened once in every thousand years, we would all
   converge
upon the tallest prospects to behold it.
It's the sunset, it's the night, it's the stars, and then
it's the beginning of another day.

Habitable Bridges

For six hundred years the buildings
were stacked atop each other on Old London Bridge,
in leaning stacks of polyhedrons that projected
out across the rushing waters
that rushed between the concrete starlings
and flowed down toward the sea.
You can hear the turning of the waterwheels
and hear the mill wheels crushing grain.
Let us walk again, to school or elsewhere,
crossing habitable bridges. On Ironsides,
the needles of the haberdasher,
the sidereal hegemony of monthliness,
to Buxtehude and toward the leaning structure,
above the candles shining through the sieves,
and the sparkling ground-glass globes
of the tea dealers' shops, the market stalls
selling huge turnips and stunning pears.
Over Southwark gatehouse, severed heads

are stuck on pikes like melons grown too ripe to eat.
Let us pause in the half-dome shelter half
of these stone pedestrian niches, to half absorb
beast fables in the clouds above the castles
that populate the sky with labyrinths
to the horizon and beyond. Let us
build our rambling houses on the bridge,
our tumbledown homes, our homes that rise
on stilts and stairs above the busy dream cafés
and restaurants of a nocturnal centennial
where the celebration will go on apace
while we are sleeping, perilously, on habitable bridges.
Life is and is not long. Let the crashing
of the waterwheels go on apace, that
you become accustomed to their crashing.
The cupolas lean out across the water.

River
Landscape

This world, its several sails,
its spires reflected on the water.
The pointed shape of a house
in sudden sunlight. From shore
where the boats rest in a small cove
an overgrown path seems to lead
into thick trees, past some barns
overgrown with ivy and flowering,
grass-covered roofs. It will be
by Prism Sunday that annulments
take effect for slanderers and parchment
handlers. Until then, be that as it may:
as a wish is full of thinking (thinking
put to flight) canal domes blue as eggshells
mark day as life in living. The wreath
of pine and holly on the wall is round
like a clock (a square clock).
The crickets begin to shrill

among the grasses of the earth.
And there among them, the pale
strawberries are more meaningful
and lovelier than hieroglyphs—
and more difficult to decipher.
As if the sky were the outer covering
of something too intimate to see
the weather-vanes point the way.
I begin my youth anew.

Batrachomy-omachia

Even through the plate-glass window
of this Chinese restaurant
with its cheap framed photograph
of jagged green cliffs
and a crystalline stairway
of foaming waterfalls leading down its slopes
even through the grime-streaked glass
of the front window
of this Chinese take-out restaurant
one can marvel at this sunset
which seems to be growing ever more grotesque
pink and terrifying above the common plane trees
rearing up in orderly arrangements
in the public park, like staves of music
composed in the twentieth century;
but look—this thing was born
in the ocean, and the ocean
is its final resting place, if rest

it will, and that I doubt
for far more likely is it that this
will dream ever sleeplessly, nervous,
trembling in the presence of a matriarch,
and will further go to show the inanthropomorphizability
of deity, and the deification of dream—
and yet more likely neither. I think
a very small grace period has been expended,
then extended, and we are enjoying
its final moments, the pink light
leveling the hedges of enclosed commons,
the gleaming sap of municipal trees—
the miscellaneous grievances have been
sapped of all their strength,
and they become finally what they always were.

The City of Magnificent Distances

Washington, DC, has been called
the City of Magnificent Distances
for its wide avenues and splendid
vistas. New Haven is the City of Elms.
And Oxford, the City of Dreaming Spires.
You must pass beneath the Bamboo Curtain
(now half eaten away by pandas)
and traverse the Great Wall to reach
the Celestial Empire. You need only
cross the Rust Belt to arrive
at the gates to the City of Brotherly
Love, where the Bell of Liberty
is waiting in its vitrine. Spread
across the Bible Belt lie the Cities
of the Plain. Like the shivering movement
of the crystalline sphere, the Windy City's

reflection shimmers on the nearly frozen lake.
Take a train along the Golden Sash
to the City That Never Sleeps,
ever watchful of its counterparts
across the water: Strasbourg, City of Bells,
and Florence, City of Lilies. The City
of Palaces is full of monuments, viragoes,
note-shavers, and centaurs. Waves lap
at the crumbling stone pilings at the port
of the City of Lamentations. Moss covers
the fallen stone arches of the Eternal City.
The City of Lanterns rises beyond the zodiac.

Famous
Androids

The Flute Player by M. Vaucanson
is one. The Chess Player by Kempelen
is also celebrated, that clockwork
visitant that stunned the Sun King's court.
There was the miniature reaper
who swung his scythe in the field
beneath a walnut shell, and then
the Lightning Concubine, ablaze
with jewels and beauty, a mechanical
cat purring in her lap. It is
the Age of Enlightenment. In the aspen grove
where the wild strawberries grow, Mr. Pope,
like a bundle of nerves in the gentle rain,
blushing in the penitential waters of the sun shower,
the ball-joint doll in petticoats is sitting
on a lichen-covered boulder. And on
the leafy ground where white-capped mushrooms
like small bells are growing all around

a brass alarm clock is ticking. New friends
come for angel visits, fireworks explode
above the reservoir and brilliant ferns
hang their bunting over crumbled fountains,
the girls are dressed like peasant girls
for lunar new year, the Day of Good Intentions
and the chiming of the Clock Symphony
violet on brick housefronts and green shutters,
a mechanical rose opens on a gold-trimmed flag
spread across a marble-topped sarcophagus.
What time is it in the forest?

Dope

I don't mean to be pugnacious,
but your bones are made of dope—
you've been x-rayed in your brindled
afghan, in your brindled cow, in your
burnoose green and fiery as a celebrant
and friend, the verdict is in: your bones
are made of dope, your blood is dope,
when you were swimming in the reservoir
down at the granite quarry, late,
in summertime, in your cruciform asymmetry,
your quince, the dense round ball,
your quince is made of dope, your sovereign
is made of dope, two pink caryatids
holding carven wheat sheaves were made
of dope, and the wheat sheaves were
wheat sheaves of freshest, vilest dope.
You live in a mansion, El Dorado,
and your mansion with its five bay windows
turned toward the bay is builded of dope
and the bay is dope, and the bodies underneath

your house turn goldener as gold doth dopeth.
Your family hath turned to dope,
and as the green piñata on your peach tree
in the courtyard spins above the children,
who hitteth it with staves, dope spills out,
the hard candy of dope, and leaves of dope
all on the ground to be gathered.

Ithaca

In the pointed shadow
of the gable, the full
grown watercress, a stream
running along the path
where the maypoles
have been erected
as if to commemorate
the indifference of the
planet, its militant
indifference, its gorges,
overgrown with tinfoil,
leafage, rusted power
trains, chokeberry, your
whole life overgrown
with the pink froth
produced in the manufacture
of soap flowing down
from the mechanized steeples
of the slumberingly
giant industrial park,

its full grown gables
and acronyms harnessing
the power of sleep
and stigmatizing it
for its uselessness.
I went down into its
gorges to watch the
sturdy watercress
the hedgehog and the badger
nuzzling the maypoles
and studying numerology
and the other creatures
in their new felt robes
testing the borders
of the wilderness,
unsure where it ended
and the city with its
bent gables and
windows hypnotized
by light began.

The Avenue
of the Hyacinth
# of Waters

One last thing
before night falls.
Dreams
are meaningless.
They are corporeal
as the corporeal violets.
They are your second
life. Your first life
has been expended
until tomorrow, when there
will be a repositioning.
Your second life
is taking place completely
outside you, in the ivies
used for decking churches
and the greened copper bronzes
of the mansards and the gambrels,

in nameless hotels
on mountainsides
where you might have stayed
once, long ago. The sky
is violet, midwinter
violet. To walk
in cold sunlight toward
the sun, almost blind,
as it shines through
leafless trees, the air
bitter and astringent
as the white root
of the water-flag
washed in coldest streams,
past the ruined buildings
and chain-link fencing
to the Avenue of the Hyacinth
of Waters and your childhood
home, or a house
that looks much like it.
These things mean nothing
when you wake.

Lepidopterans

There they are,
the lepidopterans—
they are carried
toward us on the north
wind through the strange
cloud-colored leaves
of the willow from
the City Magdalenian
where they resided
suspended temporarily
from the plumes
of the Madonna lily
and underwent a transient
clouding of consciousness
before emerging nearly
transparent into wakefulness.
You were told
one planet would influence
your whole life—but
will you let it? We open

our eyes in the glorious
uncertainty of the law
(for we are masters of its letter,
but children of its spirit).
We destroy one another.
I am full of negativity
and criticism, I sleep
beside a febrile taproot—
and they arrive
in their flowered robes
and pale purple wings:
the lepidopterans.

Gem Alphabet

The amethyst apple, first
in the gem alphabet, is precious
and inedible. The star apple
burns at the pole, as you follow
its light from the freezing trees.
The ice apple, the apple of frost, the apple
of brilliance, freezes and cracks
at the touch. If struck, the yellow
fruit of the ash apple explodes with a puff
and is reduced to its rind and a few fibers.
When the wind waged the frond war,
and a girl named Aura Freehold fled its acts,
its brilliancy, and a man named Childe Waters
held her with the gemstone of the cider,
then love was gravitation increased
or diminished, the heavy Earth
is floating in the air, the apple of grapes
is as delicious as the Apple of Body and Mind,
the yellow apple is sweet as rain
and a chill went through me when I tasted it.

Sonnet

Petrarch wrote sonnets.
So did Wyatt, and Henry Howard, Earl
of Surrey. Then came Shakespeare,
addressing his sullen, unprocreative friend
and his "dark lady." His sonnets
were good, and Helen Vendler
agrees with me. Then one day,
someone called a poem a sonnet,
but it wasn't really a sonnet.
It was just a poem with fourteen (14) lines.
Then came other irregularities,
like coats with three sleeves. Even
if this poem now has fourteen lines,
does that make it a sonnet?
Mountains, it goes without saying, have
no mothers. Neither do cities,
though they seem to need them
more than they need mayors. Cougars
stalk the borders of the vineyard
just beyond the fences. Then very

skinny poems, bones showing through,
like delicate electric fishes.
These too called sonnets. I used to
think the word was not sonnet, but
a "sonning." It still seems
to make more sense, as if pertaining
to songs, singing, sonar, solar flares.
But as for the state of sonnet affairs:
it doesn't seem like a bad thing. The Shasta daisy
shines in daylight, named by its maker
(Luther Burbank, incidentally)—anyone
is free to call a thing a sonning
just as a sunset is the end to any day.
Whether it adheres or doesn't, it goes
darkening the yellow flower, nameless
in a glacial meadow.

Hudibras

Today, in church, I wanted
to hit my kid with a cane.
He was misbehaving, naughty,
and badly needed correcting,
for in tempest, in tantrum,
to spare the rod is to spoil the child.
But what then are the specs
of aforementioned "rod" of scripture?
Does a black Oaxacan vase qualify
as "rod" if its length is greater
than its girth? And icicle tongs?
A honeydew rind, dried in sun
and braided, or length of sea-kelp
cold and washed ashore at dawn
with shards of pale pink sea glass?
Should I assume a wooden rod,
a branch clipped freshly from the pine
astud with pinecones and asway
with quills, the bluish needles
of the evergreen? What will work best

to bruise the small body of this
offender who doesn't yet know himself,
who sleeps alone in the dark scriptorium?
To discipline and punish with
a truncheon, with a net and javelin?
To confer the Midas touch with brazen knuckles?
Should the rod be iron, steel, or tungsten?
Should it be made of depleted uranium?

Portrait of
John Bours

Your white fingers
are long and delicate
and your head, bent
thoughtfully, rests
upon your fingertips
and your elbow is propped
on the polished arm
of the chair in which
you find what appears
to be momentary repose
but which is, in fact,
a carefully studied
posture—your right arm
rests casually on the back
of the chair and in
your right hand you hold
a brown cloth-covered book
embossed with red

illumination
your index and middle
fingers forming a V
upside down across
the spine and cover
just below the white
ruffles blooming like
an anemone from the sleeve
of your forest-green
velvet waistcoat
with its large green
velvet-covered buttons.
Your jacket and knee-length
breeches that button up
the side of your thigh
and end at the knee with
a narrow leather strap
and metal buckle
are the same deep green
material and the walls
behind you are covered
with this forest-green
velvet, dark and mossy.
It is not because
you are nearly smiling

that I am not convinced
that you are thinking
of the stiff volume
that you appear to have
just let fall—just look
over your left shoulder
where the window has been
flung open, or perhaps
more precisely has been
open for years and thus
these moss-covered walls—
there are trees out there
shaggy, dark, fantastic
trees, and huge clouds
billowing over their
crowns: it appears that
a storm is brewing.
The frogs you call Virginia
bells are chiming groggily
beyond the gesticulating
trees. Your natural enemies
abound. You studied
horsemanship, know
double-entry bookkeeping
speak passable French indite

verses in Latin for solemnities
keep a new brace of well-oiled
rosewood pistols in a velvet-lined
box and in the ragged
brown tobacco plants the pumpkins
and the parsnips that thrive
all too plentifully here
in this still newish world
there are flamboyant worms
in the leafage and they
are becoming the admirals
and sisters and the great purple
hairstreak who with their
red-and-purple-spotted wings
descend on the flowers
in their quintillions uncurl
a threadlike appendage
and drink from the flowers.

Remember the Telephone Book

Remember the telephone book?
It once enjoyed pride of place
in many a kitchen, in many
a breakfast nook, huge, warped
and yellow, its spine out of joint,
thicker than the Pentateuch and Septuagint,
thicker than the Ramayana, vaguely
scrofulous and antiquated even just
unwrapped from its cellophane sleeve.
You would reach for it, retrieve it
as one would pull something fully formed
from wet loam, heave it up on your knees
and it would flop open on your knees,
just a little obscenely. In its
white pages you could always find
the number for one Wolfgang Amadeus Mozart
or the street address for Clara Aufklärung;
in its yellow pages how to terminate

manhole rats or the Bridge and Tunnel
Authority, the blue pages for the offices
of governance in domed enclosures
or how to contact the sellers of tiles,
bricks, porcelain insulators,
and household crockery. And now?
Well then. It seems the telephone book has gone the way
of the top hat, the nosegay, the Automat, the rules
for auction bridge, the Hobson-Jobson
dictionary, or the plays of Richard
Brinsley Sheridan. Some printing concern,
likely in New Jersey, is printing still,
at night in a hidden maze of districts,
and some shadow courier service is bringing
them around to you; but who will have
the heavy, humble though self-serious
telephone book? You can see them stacked
like yellow cinder blocks in lobbies,
clumped in a master-block by shrink wrap
beneath the dark mail slots. A few days
later, someone just as discreetly
takes them away to an as yet undisclosed location.

The Brickyard

And I'm sick with the cold and darkness
of the unmotivational stones.
But then, it seems to hit me: they are,
after all, just stones. Oh, with what
acumen you noted that, clarified it to me
in your fashion, and not, by the way,
abstaining from your floral arguments,
your florid invective, your double entendres,
your flowery rose upon the rood of time.
So they're not the bricks in the brickyard,
beginning of a monumental tapestry
with workmen eating breakfast in the sun.
But you too were illuminated by
the general enlightenment,
in the unwithstandable century
of moment-long brightness
by a sea whose tides are calculable
but go out beneath the incalculable
sky. There was also the weeping willow
standing in the terminus and proximity

of your hypocrisy (yes, over near
the brickyard), and it was the only
real thing there among the shadow things
that also bore their fruits. And even
in the fall of rage that followed
the seasonal autumn, you could see
the leaves there, the stones there,
and settle into sleep. I have made strides
in the beckoning, not having gone against
the false salutations (yes, over
near the brickyard of the stones).
But to have grown at least at ease
and not necessarily with anything
but ease itself: nothing has happened
worth mentioning—just more flaming
gold and rectitude, viz., the setting sun,
the newly operational and ice-cold fountains
underneath which we imagined ourselves.

Tire
Manufacturers

Apollo Tyres of India.

Cheng Shin Rubber of China and Taiwan.

Hankook Tire of China and Korea.

Intreprinderea De Anvelope, Romania.

Kenda Rubber, Southeast Asia.

Michelin. Mitsuboshi Belting. Mohawk Rubber.

Panther (England), Phillips Petroleum.

Phoenix Gummiwerke, Samson, Titan Tire.

Trelleborg Gummifabriks Aktiebolag.

Uniroyal Goodrich. Uniroyal.

Hoosier, Heung Ah, Ironsides. JK Industries
of Varanasi. Armstrong, Firestone,
Gates. Universal Tire. Yokohama.

Zaklady Opon Samochodowych of Poland.

Ghosts

The first time I saw him he was standing
in front of the Iranian embassy
with his mother, or with someone I assumed
was his mother. She wore a black bonnet
like a black flower. He wore a black
frock coat and a beige collar high
under his chins. His linen
was unimpeachable. His hat
high and mighty. Mother and son seemed
to be communicating mentally, like flowers.

The next time I saw him was at the
horticultural park. His cravat was crisp
and severe as a lily. I followed him
out onto the street. He wore
a panegyric trifle in gold across his chest,
and a truffle with ruffles snapped
across his midsection. His shapely mother,
or who I assumed was same, stood beside him,
with a black lace parasol and a faded carnation.

A parade passed by, and I lost sight of them,
a parade led by a marching band
with plumed hats and flashing brass angles—
and in its midst, a float in the shape of a giant
gentleman made of flowers, his blue frock cut
from foxgloves by expert tailors,
and he loomed unsteadily above
the sparks and metal of the street.

Rapprochement

I awoke as from a dream. And I rose
near dawn, boiled and drank the blood-colored tea
sweetened with berries and wild honey,
and started to compose a lengthy list
of all of the day's necessary tasks:
a visit to the aluminum mills;
a meeting with one Solomon Mighty;
an appointment by the tall yellow gates
on the Street of the Hyacinth of Waters—
it all somehow added up to a day,
at least on paper. And as I walked out
and down a path that bordered the forest
a wind came and blew this list from my hands.
So having passed the lapis lazuli–
plated fountains and the octahedral
towers that receded to a blue prospect,
and having arrived at the green-black trees,
I decided to cut through the forest;
and having entered I could hear, just barely,
the thumping fulling hammers of the mills

of the waking city in the distance.
The primrose, amaranthus, violet
and balm; the marigold and cornflower
trembled in the zephyr. Honeysuckle
in profusion, the yellow-green vine grass
intertwined with stems of blinking daisies,
mushrooms in the deep shade of the saplings
swelling, white-yellow, with the liquor of the dew,
so unaccountable to pantheists,
seconded and blessed, the blue diurnal
water monarch and the water anarch.
And pretty soon I came to a clearing.
It was a glade, cool, green, lambent shadows
sweeping, fan-like, over lichen-covered
boulders strewn about a half-collapsed berm
with reddish vines and wide leaves of burdock,
like the ruined foundation of a house
that had been washed away in a great flood
or burned to the ground in an ancient fire.
This seemed to be the perfect place to sleep.
And as I walked toward the sunlit clearing
I noticed, half reclining in the grass,
my mother and father, a small child
playing near them in the overgrown grass.
The two were newlyweds, apparently,

young and carefree, seemingly much in love,
laughing and enjoying their small child.
They had wine and bread and green plums spread out
on the blanket where the child had gathered
a pile of polished pebbles from a stream.
They asked me to join them. I accepted,
though I knew, in some vague and quiet way,
that I had to be elsewhere, and I noticed
the rusted weather-vane standing in the grass
tied with red strips of fluttering ribbon,
and scraps of red cloth fluttering in the trees.
It was strange to think that these three people
had been here since long before I arrived,
like the trees and rocks, the stream and sunlight,
like the house that once but no longer stood,
and as I sat down to join this family
the clouds rose in great vertical towers
behind the trees as if a fire burned
uncontrolled in a faraway city.
And they were not unkind to me, only
so very involved with one another,
fascinated by and in love with the child.
And of course they didn't recognize me,
my young father, shirtless and reclining,
nonchalant and smiling in the sunlight,

my mother, slim as a willow, her hair
tied up loosely in a light blue kerchief;
both laughing and younger than the May leaves.
And me, feeling lazy and safe, a stranger
getting groggy in the afternoon heat.
I fell asleep. And later when I woke
to the sound of crickets after what seemed
like a lifetime of slumber they were gone.

Mr. Greenglass

I think I'm learning how
to write a poem. Yes, but then,
pretty soon, it seems I forget.
How is this so?
While microflora grows along
the Great Octave of pre-song thought
like water-milled green apricots
in January, Mr. Greenglass sells
his steel for sea foam,
for fresh water cinnamon.
And the trains of yellow metal
that have brought them here
pass the Northern Gate of the Sun,
pass by Christopher City.
And I have been among the men
who can be seen beside the river at midday,
drinking bottles of beer by the water
in the sunlight, living in the present.

Fireworks Display in Early Summer

They were where we went to see them:
the fireworks, near the bridge, the lit-up bridge
which is the water prism floating over
summer's river. From the crumbling parapets
that overlook the highway and the waterway
we were stirred to a kind of wakefulness
and saw them exploding, staving off the increase
of night's aloe-bladed debtors, lifting lights
skyward for love and augury's igniting.

Somewhere they are making trees pierce light
without the aid of glass, and the trapezoidal angles
of their shadows intersect. Somewhere stars
levitate above a seascape, where death laves grass
increasingly for newness. Far other sapphire-like

openings dawned upon the open visage of the rock face,
and somewhere we were granted gentle dispensations
like them, ashine for the constabulary, robed
in the monstrous burdock and the mallows,

but only in the future, like these arches, built
to be the nesting places for the starlings
of the future, like these larches, tapering into
the arches of the future, where you can rest assured
and multiform. You have heard your name called.
You are secretive like the dear earth, somehow
aligned where the grass of the body meets
the steel of the mind. Here is the garden of our efforts,
filled with lilac, leaves, lavender, summer.

Here hum the just bees of governance's apostolic
succession, in the shadows of the trees
beside the river where the crowds of young girls
flower, where evening is fanciful and dangerous,
and sunset drifted like pink smoke above the dark
and backlit cliffs, for the cliffs to share pavilions
with the winos. These fireflies and plumes of weeds
are part and parcel of the earth's good staples;
but they subvert the cloud-like animadversions

with remonstrance, with an ocean's waves of wishfulness.
This dark boat shooting missiles harmlessly
into the sky, green javelins and blue tracers
terminating in joy's strange nebulae.
Here before you is the protevangelium. It was
here before you. Here is the rose fountain,
rising, terminating, instantaneous. There are
newnesses of a familiar tint—a greenish tint
of lost familiarity; there are lavender

globes of obsolescence; and these, the floating
tactile globes of opalescence. This is a page
from the Book of Colored Shadows. And in
our prelude's aftermath we'll find our watermark,
held to the light and shining faintly through.
The voice of the community is bell-like, polyvocal,
as clear and meaningless as mountain streams,
as mountains, all laden with their virtues,
their desires, their monumentality,

the triple canopy of velvety leaves above them
that they feel compelled to move away from
to better view the distant and incendiary
sky. These blossom
technocratically above us, not the square

brick dome of an ugly precinct, nor the new
transmitter on a seminary tower, nor the brushed
metal panels on the tower's new facade;
it is the violet dome-like interior

of a giant round cactus, a skybound tunnel
ventilated with sea breezes and electric lamps.
These are big fantastic lilies gone unnoticed
by the children, because the children have disappeared
to be replaced by something else, whatever
they have grown into or out of which they have
awakened. As terra-cotta covering the blue facades
of temples, broken stone of terra-cotta,
these too re-illuminate their brokenness.

And which temple stone anticipates senility,
and which the late resurfacing of grass
that somehow antedates the oblong cloud
of a monstrous green discipleship?
As one is stirred to wakefulness by the voice
of the beloved, so I was stirred to wakefulness,
gifted with its gifts, fire's quick study, light's
fittest imp. Here beside the water prism,
where sang the rails prelusively of night,

the song that begins unduly with an opal-watered
world's beginning, an anger set to music
and projected forth by the bezeled gleam of glittering
and problematic tears, oversaturated by its famishing's
retrieval and intense assuaging, beside this bridge
this life was coming up at you as from the light.
In the thousand pages of the abstract ledger
there is an abstract version of the birth of Venus,
the other blue planet, out of which you will be asked

to memorize the platitudes verbatim, the tired
analects abiding in their worn away luster.
In this oblong box of rectangular awareness
where ovals edge against each other like the hairline
crack in Blaise's egg, they scorch the untouchable earth
with the myth of an untouchable sky. But the sky
is touchable, however violently it militates against us.
Something has been stolen from and subsequently hidden
back within the postlapsarian wilderness, and the sycamores,

like synapses, alert, are green and flicking.
And you can wear the owl's robes like the elect,
invisible inside the sycamores, and bless nightingales
with Sabbath's heiresses, the virgins gone to sleep.
The sun has long passed the meridian and there are no

shadows under the fountains. But the girls, faces lit
like apparitions under the spray of pyrotechnics,
the girls wear moccasins of dew that barely touch the earth.
This, among the telltale signs of majesty's complacence,

just as the strawberry is innocent but not good,
and man is good but not innocent, this too
can be misreckoned, and should be. What calls you
is just and exacting as Excalibur in its sharp demands,
an equalizing fire by which to tune our likenesses.
It is a fireworks display in early summer.
And we were standing by the boathouse between
the river and the forest-covered cliffs
with light showering down all around us

as if Persephone were handling the radical grapes
of wine with ice-cold gloves. But she was not.
We were drinking the wine to make us radical with love
under trees where glaciers once, millennia ago,
were de-iced by grace's own raindrops. We were standing
on the earth, this heavy ball of earth and granite,
iron and basalt, of mountains, streams, and seas
that nonetheless was floating through the air
with a gentle and abiding forgetfulness.

Song

Nevertheless, the cardinals practice
their speech above the Saugerties,
the white elms listen.
Cranes come down from
the gables, rare and wet
as cresses washed by rain
in the primal garden.
So you wandered there
with the wild birds
your breasts like yellow plums
your whole hair-raising childhood,
and listened to them sing for you:
A dark blue one for
the Past. One speckled
brown and green for the Present.
A sky-blue one for the Future.

Nineteenth-Century Novel

Read me that story all the way through,
the one about the undisciplined, showy daughter
of a self-made man, who lived on Green Lettuce Lane
in Clovernook in a house with a green
lattice gate. This daughter, Miss Cornflower,
would be flighty and rude until one day carried off
by a rake, one Charles Bronzely.
It is cold in deep space, and the planets
are the Children of the Mist, shy children,
and the Bride of the Sea is a chilly bride,
gowned in green seaweed, a demon.
Bridges of cane are thrown over narrow streams
and will make do, as well as rainbow bridges.
But how long and how far will she run
with her fashionable lover, cruel, ghastly,
and fascinating? The setting is embroidered
with a thousand many-colored flowers
and silver streams and hyacinth on waters

and this man of bronze meanders with his broad grin
through the peaceable kingdom. Yet soon enough
a distant prospect of the city is apparent
through the trees. Even here, now,
violet clouds reflect the city lights.
It is double summer for the lake guns
on the far shore, which are the smokestacks,
the lotuses of heavy industry, the pell-mell
velvet facings that whet the blades
on the exchange economy, asbestos batting
pouring forth from late demolished structures
and pink froth from the culverts.
And how long will this daughter hold her hand
to the stove in the subpassages of foundries?
How long will the air castle hover, green-shielded,
in its gargantuan curriculum? If we study
the curvature of domes, will we rise up
into their spaces, spaces flowering with emptiness,
or the sharp cavernous splendor of the pine forest?
But look—what used to be a stone tower
is half collapsed, a tree grows out of the ruins.
Our boat is just drifting along through the blue-green water
past them.

River Running
by a Glassworks

The poet falls asleep. In this
he is doing his work. The cormorant
dips her head in the water, then
goes under the water completely.
It was all right to be wrong
if among the least embroidery of dew
that chilled the leaves of flowers
a piercing negligent reluctance
to its intransigent necessity
was piercing as the raindrops.
(And it is raining on the glassworks.)
The river is the same once, the same
twice, the same thrice, in as many different ways.
In this it is the same river.
It is the same river as the poet
is the same sleeper when he wakes
beside the river, the river
running by the glassworks,

the glassworks blinking in the rain,
the rain the same rain falling
on the aforementioned cormorant.
They have done their work, for the moment,
and they can rest now.

Biography

This life is the emergency we have to face. —HANS KÜNG

Of his schooldays we know little.
He was riding the back of a swan.
He was riding the back of a monkfish
Through the fiery portals of dawn.

Of his childhood less is known.
But damage had been done.
He was flopping up a fish ladder
In a halfhearted effort to spawn.

Of his arbitrage much has been written
On foolscap marbled with dew.
Having traveled edgewise through icebergs
He was turned like a case-hardened screw.

He was, one might say, born anew.
He had touched a fiery throne.
His hand suffered 3rd-degree burns
That seared through to the bone.

Bondage and destiny blazed.
He sipped the cold crabapple juice.
His effigy, burning, was raised
Over the town and turned loose.

He felt like someone else.
Orange pylons turned in the sky.
They seemed so much braver than he—
A thing merely shrinking and shy.

A blue flame smoldered and hissed
On each end of his two-tone mustache.
The white flames of day were approaching.
He fell down to earth with a splash.

His feet touched the rubbery floor
And cold lettuce fields of the sea.
He bobbed up and washed ashore
With the delicate foam and debris.

He crawled toward a stand of palms.
A blue crab hung from his nose
By one lean and smiling claw.
He crossed his eyes and froze.

He was riding the back of a swan.
He was riding the back of a dream.
He was hopping from ice floe to ice floe
On a thawing, half-frozen stream.

One chunk of ice broke away.
He stood on its marble floor.
The blue crystal oblong swam
Toward the tall purgatorial door

Of day. No,
Night. No, day's
Own trees aglow
In magic rays.

Was he any more human now?
He seemed to be in one piece.
One appendage hung limp from his shoulder
Glazed with a brownish grease.

Light was upon him now.
He crawled toward the buildings of ice.
The horizon flung up auroras.
They told him to arise.

Their voices came from afar.

They rose and died on the wind.

They were faint as a morning star.

They said goodbye to him.

The Island of
the Blessed

On the Island of the Blessed,
so they say, the apples
are always within reach, violet,
ever ripe. So why do you wake up
each night, your mind racing
in the dark? Count to one thousand,
count a thousand lambs in pastures,
a thousand angels, count a thousand
archangels, count a thousand Seraphim,
Cherubim, Powers, and Thrones
until the Seychelles are clearly visible.
On the Island of the Blessed they watch
the play of waves, the play of waves
and roses, trefoil, and lavender are
growing blossoms the size of human heads
along the paths leading down to the water.
You have been wondering where your life
is leading. You will be a widower

and an orphan, you will lose everything—
in the steady current you can feel
an undertow. Dominions, Virtues,
Principalities. The apples, half purple
speckled with green, half green flecked
with purple, some are clustered on the boughs,
and some lie rotting underneath the tree—
others still are piled in this
glazed and fired earthenware bowl
each a small taste of the island
from which they came.

Away, in the Change That Befell

Were we to learn that we too were subject
to the lean, animal satisfactions
of the parables, the snow parable
and the parables of sand and thistle
when in fact the mystery of what was meant by them
never came up—we sat, dined in silence.
The house cat turned into a small, black gem.
We communicated in the idiom spoken
by some petty bureaucrat millennia ago,
on some other continent, a spired
and jasmine-fragrant continent
where it seemed the rye of futurity was withering
under a hail of incandescence,
the fail-safe mode that leads to mental stalemate,
metal grass for coriander bees.
And sometimes, like them, we just raised

ghost propositions, let them float there
momentarily, irrelevant. Then we dined
on salad made from smallage, wild celery,
water parsley, while you were away, in the change
that befell, and walked the path in the darkness
of pines, not hunting for black mushrooms
nor for the gold mushrooms of the sea
but for the cool shade of the pines subterranean,
the beautiful hotel among the colored mosses.
We paused and looked around us,
and the grass was damp with sweet
delicious dew beneath the morning bridges.
A dome of clouds is glowing over the tinted trees:
of course it's not what you thought it would be,
it's looming unintentionally
above you, shadowing you, it legislates,
unknowing, sacralizing tears, pearls, salt columns,
urns of rainwater, its interlunar vacancy—
its causes are unknown, but its effects are more
than apparent, they are present,
and inscrutable. Lights are in the trees
above the stone guardhouse.
It's a time for celebration—the man
who has lost something finds it again
in an unexpected place—the place most

obvious. And buildings, tall as wheat sheaves
on the Sabbath lean into the light for harvest,
and hayricks for perennials where scythes
see fit to stand apart and shine.
The table is set. The plates gleam, the glasses
brimming with wine or cold, clear water gleam,
and a hand on my knee felt like an abject
and implacable criticism: the night is long,
but so is the day, and you are in a trance
and they are equalized and full of mercy.
It has told its innocent and ancient tale.

Men of the Twentieth Century

They are wearing suits and knitted ties
and thick overlapping overcoats
that fold upon their coats of worsted wool
and double breasts. And they are wearing
doves darkened by the night, and caps
with brims that snap, their hair
streamlined with brilliantine and bronzish-
green. Their satchels bright
with beaded rain hold scores symphonic,
as they pass through the double doors
of *metamorphosen*.
                 Henceforth
shall we all sit down in the woods
and marvel at their fortune?
Their prevailing is the simplest prevailing:
to have grasped the water-damaged spine

of a biography, to have carved out a self
from among all others, as from cliffs,
that become transparent as water,
Shostakovichian as transparency
is shocking, as clearly visible
as they come striding up to us
aroused from furtive and sporadic rest
at long last: willing and accountable,
alive in their banality, in cubical,
in stadia, in firestorm, in chancellery,
the men of the twentieth century.

Shadow Government

With its buildings round as orient pearl
and senators in silken headgear—
while in small cities underground
the animals are in their warrens,
maze-like, our shadow siblings—
this modern world is edging forward
with the zeal of wishful thinking,
with Mother Wit, as full of gems
and evil magic as the Arbuthnot Anthology,
wolves, concubines, and harvesters,
the great yellow disc harrow resting
in its rust on the outskirts. In the center
sophists practicing a silken homiletic,
our fictitious sibling, our shadow
trustees in the buildings round
as dewdrops, while in small cities
within a city, small as dewdrops,
a shadow government is preparing
to govern.

Clematis

Now that the maximalists have spoken,
and now that the maximalists are here
and they have polished the classical arch
to a uselessly gleaming whiteness
while still the human eye is picking out
the specificity of grass and metal in the sunshine;
the steel-blue apples hanging heavy on the tree,
the bottle-green paper—one sheet and one leaf—
and now that the tropes have been exploited
on the tall illuminated billboards
let us turn our attention briefly toward
the green pearlescent night, the Heaven of Pearl
and its heavy book wherein the names
of the newly born are ever being written
in the spaces that the newly dead have left;
the green and alabaster night, whose banisters
are leading down to the water, where the paymaster
seeks his brief repose beside a silent
apparatus. That would be the clematis,
whose red vine is washed with icy water,

but will sing, after all, her aria at daybreak
but will not reflect the mirror image of her innocence
in opening. Under the cliffs, where the school
for machinists conducts its daily lessons,
slim lampposts curve above the train tracks.
Pink bales of Thermafiber on the freight cars,
and here a sheet of crumpled blue metal
amid the dry and fallen leaves, the metallic
cry of the jay, the peeling yellow paint
of the conducting towers kindled in the nascent grass.
When all things have grown plain and clear
(as they will, for it is night—round and clear
as orient pearl, translucent sunflower of the waters)
no longer will the swung dash need to come before
each main entry in the lexicon, a star ablaze
above the lemongrass lest you misreckon.
When day comes, with warmer weather,
the mounted police, their sky-blue helmets shining,
come toward us from the trees, then disappear
into the foliage, just as abruptly, once again.
And we can follow them into the forest,
to where a glass bottle has left its
bottle-shaped impression in the interwoven grass,
and the violet clematis blooms beside
a concrete berm stained red with oxidation.

Here is where the night will come to its fruition,
just reclining here inside itself with the green
pearlescent forest, through whose leaves the city's
abstract lights are shining from a distance,
night winding down, night orient, night contemplative.

The Trap

A rat got into the house.
It ran across the floor.
I couldn't get the rat.
It was a compact rat.

It wasn't a Holstein rat
with udders the size of a cat.
Which offered some consolation.
It was, nonetheless, not not a rat.

I set about making a trap.
It involved a box and a beam,
a grape and a length of string
all set in a frame like a loom

and sent into motion by steam.
It was angular, deadly, pristine.
It was tall and filled most of the room.
The rat was nowhere to be seen.

The house rose up all around
the trap that was poised to spring.
The trap was an awesome machine.
It no longer needed the rat.

It was sensitive to sound
and every move I made
so I moved through the house with care.
I tried not to raise an alarm.

I sat on a chair very still.
I tried not to make it afraid.
It seemed to work like a charm.
I no longer needed the trap.

Venus Victrix

We were rooting for Mustafa Hamsho.
On the other side was Marvelous Marvin
Hagler. They were two rounds in, and Hagler's hook
was mountainous as Fuji, his jab an ordeal,
a trial by hammer and tongs. Hamsho attacked,
disorderly; there seemed to be a method,
albeit a secret one, a sort of sable
methodism. Once in a while they hugged
like bears at spawning runs while rainbow trout
flopped over rocks under the aurora borealis;
and oddly, an aurora borealis of fragrant rings
from the wet cigar smoke rose into the lights.
"They're bugbears, all right," intoned one mobster,
touching, for comfort, his Luger in its shoulder holster.
Hagler was serving up raw knuckle sandwiches,
the most undelicate of finger foods.
Hamsho threw grappling hooks across the chasm
aiming for the crenellations of his rival's grizzled brow.
At round's end, Hamsho goes to his corner
like a schoolboy asked to wear the dunce cap.

Enter leggy playthings in bikinis.
Round three is Canto Nine, so clang the bellwether.
The prostitutes are tangible and marvelous
as tiger stripes, so pass down the cigars.
Presently Hamsho, ordinarily a biped,
is temporarily a quadruped—the Syrian
is acting out the answer to the riddle of the Sphinx
in a most accomplished pantomime.
Hagler's arms are swinging, two wrecking balls,
two orbs of pain-delivering titanium—
that futuristic, yes, but prehistoric
in their lobster-claw ferocity.
With scissor hands that soon are pinking shears
pruning round the topiary of Mustafa's
battered countenance, Hagler works upon those hedges,
forming a swan and a myrtle fleur-de-lys,
suitable for nymphs and pretty butterflies
such as those now fluttering about the head of Hamsho.
When Hamsho falls a second time, his mentor,
Hamsho's name ablaze across his satin jacket,
intercedes—an act of mercy. Now, Hagler,
you are rightfully called Marvelous, a lion
in Garden Americana.

King of
the Dudes

What kind of father would dress
his newborn baby girl as a Victorian
English gentleman and call her
Mr. Wopsle? I am aghast.
A triple-breasted vest, you say?
A frock coat and a wide cravat?
What did he hope to gain from this?
Does a vague resemblance to Benjamin
Disraeli or a railroad baron
better ensure a hasty weaning?
Will she more readily master Mandarin?
Did he name her Quentin Crisp
or Evander Berry Wall? Is she
a little plutocrat, an Oscar Wilde
amongst the puppies?
Did he walk her through
the Crystal Palace while she twirled
a silver-knobbed cane?

And was she garbed in a startling striped shirt
in red and sky blue, wide trousers
tapered at the ankle, and white spats?
It was a dirty trick akin to
mango showers, cashews in iced
coffee, root beer on the roots
of redwoods. A top hat wreathed
in wintergreen, sea bream, shaving
cream. With a fob watch (what?!),
yes, a fob watch that told the
time twice in Jakarta, and the cricket
scores in Lahore and Rawalpindi.
You have over-starched her collar,
yes, you've over-starched the Egyptian
single-stitching of her collar.
I will see you in court—and not
a court of squash or Basque pelota—
if you will, a court of law,
a royal or imperial court
where they will place this lovely
child, this erstwhile little gentleman,
atop the grand piano
beside a Ming vase overflowing
with chrysanthemums.

The Lackadaisical Poets

Nothing stands between you and the poem—
a wave of sisterly benevolence
nearly a mile high. And you need to choose
a subject: exile, for example, rain,
or blue-chalk systems of analysis
that incandesce above the red-clad cities.
Spiders of sisterly analysis
are spinning their webs in the red cities.
And clouds of brotherly love are building
their appurtenances above the fretted iron gables
and caverns measureless to man
down to a sunless sea. And mermen
leaning drowsily against each other
on benches in front of the windmills.
Have they come here to be near you?
Have the cypresses, high and pointed,
asway behind the gables, come to entertain you?

And Proteus arising, new as glass,
to dream day's dream anew?
You've been wandering some scary neighborhoods
in earshot of the Wordsworthian sea,
spiderwebs enormous in the sunlight
and wires hanging from the tall bare poles
of the abandoned manzanita nursery.
Let us turn our thoughts then
to the lackadaisical poets,
the crickets in the long stems,
and the dew in the Hippocrene stems
as April, when spray beginneth to spring,
falls over the dark, Virgilian hives,
and the green biplanes, the new crop-dusters
hum above the yearlings. And the pinkish mist
that trails behind them comes to rest
like dew upon the rupees, and the land,
the brown and gentle land, the patterned
cultivated land, a problem for the Directorate
of Waterways to solve, is as simple and fragile
as the glassine geodesic domes amid the feldspar.
Now everything you seize will be unknown to you,
at least for the moment.
That they might become as children yet again,
a mere cloud drifting in the sunlight.

Purple Martin

They come to us suddenly and are not yet ours.
They come fully formed.
As the gray steel cables of the bridges
appear threadlike from a distance,
the new green leaves are uselessly alive.
Behind the angular blue-gray buildings
the cloud-like mountains rise into the sunset.
And that is the other metropolis.
Life enters there, like children's hair,
suddenly changing, from light to dark
and back again. And that makes us adroit,
and wanting to be human—that is, something
somehow other than ourselves. The absinthe
handlers and the water lobsters in the brine,
the foyer painted black with golden leaves
of rococo design; the lilies and the sea-waves
come; they come, they come to us, and we
have met them with the mystery of what we are.
Yes, Herr Rektor, Man is not a hammer,
and the mind is no machine, and the scalloped

shapes of basins under fountains have no function.
Look: a form rising up above the tops of trees
in April blossom: Martin Heidegger
has fallen asleep in a pinkish cloud
of rain and dew.

Prelude to What Comes Next

Knives may be sharpened on ivy roots,
willow, and holly. Seaspray does not injure
sycamore or tamarisk. Grass will grow
beneath the alder, ash, plane, and sycamore
but not the aspen, beech, chestnut, and fir.
Chestnut and olive never warp. The unmoving
cloud that seems to billow on the cyclorama,
the dream, the waking day, the rain-wet leaves.
Condensation builds up on the windows.
Bankrupt and in the Exchequer's black books,
you've inscribed the Ramayana on a tetrahedron
about the size of a dreidel. It's okay.
Through the sky fall fire-threaded hats
for rectors, plums with streaks of green
and violet, beetles with green markings.
You came to her first as a child,
then as a lover, then as a litigant.
Is this the prelude to what comes next

(low as it may be on the scale of verities)?
As a ptarmigan lays aside its winter plumage,
lay your burden down beneath the trees,
in the cool shadow of the moss: your life
will be there still when you awaken,
like a grape-colored ribbon laid across
the tinted page of a book that you have closed.
Then when you return, touchstone, opal
of the pale, a child fully human in your wakefulness,
full in your adulthood as absinthe for the weary,
as fortitude for tedium, the lesser agons:
we could be drinking ice wine right now,
made from the grapes we left to freeze
on the silver branches at dusk. We could
be new, beautiful, appeased, immortal.
Or watching the Orange River thaw
as it flows through Mönchengladbach at dawn.

Buddha

The world's largest seated bronze Buddha
is green, like a rooftop in an old city
where rain is falling with its ancient sound,
where men in topcoats hurry past the ministries
with the craggy shapes of bustards staring down,
and its face with its half-closed, heavy-lidded
eyes is stamped on red tablets—is he sleeping?
Is he growing angry with us in the cities,
judging from his throne in pink haze, watching
men gnaw the touchstone, watching men nibble
the scraps of governmental largesse?

For we have been given, and have been given
pepper spray and electricity, tigresses
and near invisibility; the eight-day clock,
red-tape protocols, the rotatory calabash;
and a seven-foot tall lath and plaster hat
mounted on wheels and dragged along
the boulevards—and he is giant, stone,
and tranquil and angry as a flower, as a flame,

a statue of liberty in full lotus. What would it take
to make him stand? Once upon a time
the world's largest standing Buddhas
were standing at timeless attention
in their niches in the Afghanistan cliffs.

Who thought vigilance could look so like peace?
Let us say an angry *Shanti* as they pass.

The Petronas Towers

I've always felt that lobsters and snow crabs
and other large marine crustacea
should be considered terrifying. What are they,
after all, if not giant spiders, spiders
as large as a dog or a human child?
And they are weaponized with claws
and pincers honed over the millennia.
Every i should be dotted with the smallest
facets toward completion, crescents should suggest
the circle, full and ripe as cantaloupe
growing on the vine, which, in turn, suggests
and promises delicious nectarine slices
which, after all, are crescents perfect
and symmetric as the two Petronas Towers.

But the Petronas Towers lean in the Malaysian sky,
shining, jagged on their surfaces and full
of quantitative hedge funds where geniuses

are crunching numbers, cooking books,
and bottling the nectar. You can walk
from one to the other on the sky-bridge
that connects them, that allows the tall Petronas Towers
to comfort one another, join hands with one another,
for they are lonely up there,
blooming and ablaze in the metallic sky.

Rose of
Sharon

Do me a favor.
I want you to crack that egg
against the side of my head
and then prepare it and feed it
to me. I also want you to equate
mastery with mimicry,
and to equate confusion of the two
with equation. The evening grosbeak
has settled on a branch of hawthorn.
A line of verse is not a rope bridge
flung across a chasm. A tree
in the downpour infringes on
my sense of self.

When the *Lusitania* could sail
unchallenged, a ball-shaped ghost ship
in defiance of all shadow enemies,
of all shadows, and the purple

chains of Alpine valleys
were blue with the blossoming
glory-of-the-snow, and in
the intervening years, turnips
tall as houses, swarms of venomous
frogs, monstrous children
bearing grown-up bodies;
under the eel-colored sky
a great sheaf of orange fungus
blooms atop a fallen log.
Listen, Poet: you can't bring in
two consecutive pieces from the junkyard
of desire—it is a mismanaged junkyard.
You must separate them with
an interval—a purely bureaucratic
interval in which you can let
all things be done unto edifying.

Invective
Against Pugs

People with babies
are as strange as people
with pugs. Pugs, so small
and ugly, baby-like,
inexplicably decked out
or dolled up in their
little sweaters, their
masters and mistresses
bending down
to greet each other's
pugs and revealing
deep cleavage as if
to excite each other's
pugs. Some people
put their pugs into
frilly perambulators,
old-fashioned baby buggies
for their pugs, make them
don lace bonnets and pink

satin bibs—some have been known
to put top hats on them,
like little Victorian gentlemen.
Are they changelings? Did goblins
put the pug here in place
of a real human baby?
No, by God, there is
no baby, just pug
or pugs. You think,
did the pugs suffer
in some great war
or tragic conflagration?
What then have they done
to earn such comforts?
For you, my friends,
are spoiling your pugs.
Their faces (the pugs'
I mean) bespeak familiarity
with some profound
and undefined suffering.
Yet despite
a sometimes lacerating
empathy, the pugs maintain
a stoic acceptance
of that injustice and that

suffering. But you
would be wrong to be fooled
by these appearances.
Indeed, like beautiful boy
fashion models who sullenly
lay across each other's
knees in leather riding
boots and wear tweed
swallowtail waistcoats,
whose blonde locks flop over
their eyes in the drawing
rooms of British manor
houses with many gables
and who (I am only
imagining now what they
might be doing) perhaps
lick cocaine from a pewter
dish, the pugs merely cultivate
a look of stylish boredom.
The pug: what is he thinking
really? About biting a rat
in half or a girl pug, I'd wager,
or maybe smoking a pug cigar.
Sometimes I see someone
with a pug and that air

of self-satisfaction and I want
to say to them: "Hey, do you think
you're the first person
on Earth to ever have
a pug?" I'm sorry, but you just
can't teach your new pug
Mandarin.
In my estimation
pugs are OVERRATED.
Put all the pugs on a boat
with pit bulls, send them off
into the sea, then let
the pit bulls eat the pugs.
Then let high-voltage
eels stun the pit bulls,
and piranhas eat the pit
bulls. Then as the pugs flee
the tripes of the pits
and dog-paddle back to shore
let the eels re-stun the pugs.
I've had my say.
That is all for now.

The Lilies
of the Field

Are my fears really groundless?
Should I just consider the lilies of the field?
Or should I be desperately, tirelessly, fiercely
attempting all day to make something of myself
much like these others here at the cubical farm—that could be.
That black-haired female figure on the train
perused the New York Sun so gorgeously
I could give myself to how such permanence purls forth
in beads of song, like leaves, like leaves
from the Song of Songs and then is gone.
I don't know what these people are busy doing all day,
but they face their tasks with deadly gravity
and seem in a great hurry to see them done.
Many of them talk like Navy colonels, or admirals.
Others try hard not to sound like admirals—
they're more like three-star generals in bearing.
I overhear one vice president of some department on a
    conference call:

he's asking for, or rather demanding, a "rough roadmap
of how we're going to proceed." What's that mean?
Well, he's not asking for a valentine, or a puppy!
The guy on the other end of the line is frozen stiff—
he doesn't have a clue how they're going "to proceed."

They're telling me it's no stigma to be
an office clerk in a glassworks, though far
from the fire, and far from the autumn
fire of the great rose windows.
A persimmon is floating in the watercooler,
and I am jerked awake by its astringence.

From here (the 47th floor) you can see for miles.
You can see China—well, a teacup made in China—
large on the horizon, just beyond New Jersey.
A man down on the street (something of a dandy,
I propose) wears a stovepipe hat of more than average
circumference, large enough for a man to fit in,
large enough, in fact, to hide a whole family in.
Ah, wrong again: "he" is the McGraw-Hill Building,
the old, green, deco one, covered in blue-green terra-cotta.
And yet on second look, there is someone down there
and he is dressed as a stovepipe, with a stovepipe hat,
Abe Lincoln–style, and stovepipe trousers,
and he's smoking a stovepipe for good measure.

                                        I daresay
I'm feeling a little beleaguered. Thankfully
I'm somewhere else now. I'm walking beside a pond.
It's better. Willows loom colossal in the sunlight.
Now, to let this cool wind blow on my face
for just a moment, not thinking about work
or money or poetry. And then I am reading
the Upanishads, and I don't understand them.
Up there in the sky, the world is a fire,
up there where we don't belong,
the raincloud is a fire, the earth
is a fire, man is a fire, water comes to have
a human voice, and all speak, for God
the Onlooker is on the inside looking out
but seeing, somehow, into us.

When I awoke as from a revery
the white trees cast their shadows
on the interlocking stones
of the pathway, grown men in long
paisley gowns rode past on tall blue tricycles,
and workers gathered for tea and cold lunch
from crystal mess kits under the statue
of the Unknown Citizen. A few men
in uniform slept beside a stream.

The Problems
of Poetry

I love to see how other people
have solved the problems of poetry.
Sometimes it blinds me
like rock gloves landing on my hat.

Other times it seems both still
and ever spreading, as the tendrils
of a grayish potted aloe
in the window of a dry cleaners

on a narrow hilly street.
Still other times it is like the vacant lot
behind the hill beneath the trestles
of an elevated building—

in the leafless brown undergrowth
behind the chain-link fencing
lie the rusting hubcaps, spackle cans,
broken kitchen cabinets, an engine

covered with a blue plastic tarp,
broken umbrellas, propane tanks,
cinder blocks, upended fireplugs,
dead brown vines and balls of aluminum foil,

a rotting log crawling
with millennial centipedes and centennial millipedes
among the man-made hats of paraphernalia.
They are chaste as berries and mortality,

sand runes in an eclogue, the stoic
wolves of absolute winter. It is
but a short walk to the shining gray-tiled pillars
of the housing project.

Dream of January

FOR HIROAKI SATO

I'm sitting under a tree   Eating a mushroom   The size of a
    human head.

Street lined   With green, archaic theaters: The will has been
    tested.

Green peeling paint   On the seaside retaining wall—   Five
    different interleaving greens.

A grapefruit, tremendous and discolored,   Growing soft amid
    the grasses   Of a vacant lot.

Darkness,   Let the abstractions   Come to play.

In dream, I keep   Rolling double fives   On trapezoidal dice.

Rebuild   the World Trade Center   In a cornfield full of crows.

Man wearing ear piece   Steps on centipede   And walks on.

Just beyond the building's shadow: Parking lots overgrown
   With yellow-green thistle.

A cricket   Chirping   In my children's dark bedroom.

In dream my mother has a twin   And I can't tell the difference
   Between them.

Ladies and gentlemen,   These grapes   Are hospital grapes.

Black plums.   Asian pears.   Blue concrete.

In the oblong book   The recipes   Involving fungus.

Flakes hanging   From the water-damaged hotel ceiling—
    I forgot my dream.

I read the Book of Knots   To the attentive taproots   In the
    evening chill.

Dream of January: Dirty cobwebs   Hanging from the trestles
    of an aqueduct.

Steady your nerves—   Electricity comes to us   By waterfall.

Coltish   Girlish, green   Playful saplings.

Merely a carrot would be fine—   As long as it's organic   And
    carved into a futurist swan.

At six months   The expectant mother's womb   Is the size of
a melon.

Bad lunch: One raw tentacle   On a Styrofoam plate.

Giantesses—   Nimbus clouds   Above the ghost town.

As the anesthesia wears off   It dawns on me: My surgeon is
a water beetle.

The seashore at dawn: Polished glass and driftwood in the
sand,   A giant jellyfish, blue and trembling.

The greenish clouds   Seem calm and cool—   Then the
luminous, giant raindrops.

With crickets chirping   By our heads,   The cool, yellow lichen.

Baby centipedes   And baby humans   Coexisting uneasily.

This will be the year   I grow my mustache long   And start
    inviting freaks to tea.

Sundowner smoking in the lindens: so be it.   Teak for the deep-
    toned cribbage board: so be it.   Votary glass aslant the water
    mill: so be it.

The infant's errand: Desolation   For the young mother.

A brand   Of condoms   Called Misty Pavilions.

The radical   Sharpens his pencil   The same old way.

Winter   Foxes   Stillborn in the evergreens.

Two girls whispering,   Face-to-face,   Foreheads nearly touching.

Who is your birth mother?   Yellow clouds   Roll toward the sea.

Knitting a sweater   Whose sleeves trail   Out the door, down
    the stairs, out to sea.

There was a boy—   Raindrops   Glittered in the foxtails.

Shaving off my sideburns   In a dim casino restroom   In the
    dream.

In the open air market,   Boxes of bluish apples   And tiny, alien
    pears.

Summer solstice—   I walked all the way to the sea   In tin foil
    rain boots.

The yellow hammer calls: "Come down from the masts.
    Walk five abreast in the sun."

A dream from childhood: Swimming naked   Near the huge,
    ancient ruins.

The bad boy   Sleeps   In the golden poplars.

Eating foot-wide noodles   With clairvoyants   At the posh
    seaside resort.

Nature is whimsical.   I am dressed   Like a girl.

Man strokes   Beard. Child   Strokes cat.

Pregnancy test: Blossoming plum branch   Shining with rain
    water.

Miltonic windmills   And steel mills   In the dawn.

Children breaking   Man-made laws   In flowered dresses.

Dream: Man.   Darkness.   Robots.

Eels breeding   In the silver water   By the smokestacks.

Five new yellow peppers,   Heads bent   Thoughtfully.

The oval.   The ovum.   The underwater picture window.

Children: Bushels of fire   In the dawn.

Sit in the dark.   Rest for a while.   Jellyfish fill the sea.

Across the water—   Another beautiful city   Just like this one.

Victory
Gum Ball

The gum ball rolled down the ramp
made of lead and laid at an acute angle
on the hillside, down, down it rolled.
And it rolled down the rain-damp ribbon roads
and out of town and past the dump
whose rusted-out and saber-toothed projections
lit amber lamps in the moss pits
and still it rolled. And it was not
a cue ball or an earthen lump
nor aspirin nor a game piece
nor a limousine of ideation,
lime-green as a fireball.
It was not a caplet of striped niacin.
Though these might have seen or felt
the caress and light of its rolling,
for it was an albino, touched with whiteness
where grape or melon-colored coverings
should have otherwise beset our watching

like birds in the dawn-reddened gables.
The oil derricks tottered in the bay, unaffected,
unafraid, but then it rolled down into the grass
and past a stump, where things turned ugly,
for the lumpen proletariat encamped there
vowed to stomp toward progress, a world
including not our sweet and useless ball of sugar icing.

The Altar Boys

I spoke to Mother,
and my dreams repeated back to me
seemed childish and insincere.
As a young man cites his past as altar boy
to help lend credence
to his unbelief, was I too
rigging Santa Claus to willow masts
and stripping him to help make
kindling burn the tracts
of old Duns Scotus? Look, you,
I can play poet with the best of them.
And look, Mom, this poet
was drunk on the wine of Heaven,
at war with giantesses in the clouds.
Yes, grown men still trade emeralds
for emirates, sell the bitter color
off the bitter red gentian,
gallant men, men of power, men
of purpose. But a boy beside an altar
holding up a golden book for lectors—

who is he? When and how will he
become himself? When he too
is a man? And what is that?
He will cry for his mother
while he denies his father. His heart
will be buried in the earth . . .
where it will grow. His head
will be in the sky, where the air
is pure and cold.

Mountain Man

The mountain man had a shaggy mane
of hair and a shaggy beard,
and he lived on the side of a mountain
at the higher elevations of the mountain
and did his yeoman's work that being
a mountain man entailed:
he made his own cheese, and kept it cold
in an icy brook, he hunted fish
with a javelin of his fashioning
and stood upon a moss-covered rock
like some Pythian Apollo
and let it fly into the cold water
and as the sun went down he carried
his basket of rainbow-colored people
of the finny tribe back toward
his shack, which stood like a good-sized plug
of shag tobacco in a stand of trees;
and at night he would smoke his pipe
with his feet up on a stump
while smoke drifted up through

a tin-can chimney, so his whole house
from outside looked like an ember
in the bowl of a smoldering pipe.

Mountain man, far be it from me
to begrudge you this piece of paradise.
You speak French with the foxes,
English with the elk, and American
with the crude and dirty bears.
You wear a big hat of pinecones.
You look like a mountain,
and every day, the mountain
looks more and more like you.
But down below, beneath the crags
and the knobby windswept alders
on the northern face, and down
beneath the glaciers at the slopes,
there in the fields and the farms
around the windmills and the steepled towns
the Great War is raging.

The Task

Here are the names of apples:
Empire. Gala. Northern Spy.
And what of the Lapis Lazuli?
If you can tell A from gables

then here is the door, there is the way.
Strew green rushes for the stranger.
Abandon palace glass to archers.
The gaudy boats of coming day

are boats of morning and arrive
unlikely as a green frost,
an effect without a cause, caused
by its very own being. I've

seen how everyone becomes a child
in the snow, and innocent in sleep
and how the blue garlic-bulb shapes
of temple domes in sunlight, blue-tiled,

are magnified through the spyglass
of a dream, and how their towers
appear with the minutiae of mosaic flowers
made from bits of tile and broken glass.

Are we in Denmark, then? The rose damask
is native to streets paved with ice.
The clock tower tells the hour twice:
in its tolling; in its shadow; this its task.

Beholder

The big yellow cauliflower of the fungus
split open at the bottom of the culvert.
The cold water is flowing over it
and into the waterlogged bales of hay
that circumscribe the cinder block catch basin
at the bottom of the culvert.
The big yellow fungus, roughly the size
and shape of a human head, has little,
if anything, to tell us. It just lets
the cold water flow over it. The yellow
fungus is in the eye of the beholder.
The yellow fungus is the beholder.
The leaves are green as crystals of the sea
in the mind of the beholder, in whose
intractable mental arrangements are formed,
cloud-like, not only the present, and past,
but even an alternative past, wherein
ball clover thrives, velocipedes are moving
gracefully, an antique locomotive is puffing
far beneath a fleet of humming airships,

passing through the clouds above this fair isle,
where the Martello Towers are mushrooming
serenely, and where these ruined pavilions
in the cliff sides are once again agleam with silver,
and fragrant with coffee and spices.
The mandarin pears outweigh the Brahman apples
in their sweetness. And in those green-tiled domes,
how the shadows of the lilies fall among the candles,
the vitality and strangeness of that contrast
ever obscuring their slide into diminishment.
It has taken you through corridors of light
and shadow, and halls of blue mosaic tile,
and from there has taken you into its counsel
where, beside the waterfall, you can hear
the rain drumming on the burdock leaves.

The Metaphor

The Metaphor of Life:
some call it a sea, or a stream
or a path. Some call it
a mountain stream, or an underground
path, and others just call it
a path. And there are pitfalls
that mark the metaphorical path
you're treading, including serpents
banded with gold and purple,
butterflies in dark trees
and reapers in fields of glittering corn—
they are part of the metaphor, too.
In the bare branches of a hedge
small speckled birds with scarlet
plumage, and the smooth, yellow-green
body of the female cardinal,
and beneath the hedge the small pale leaves
of the dittany of Crete, the apple mint,
the rue, the herb-of-grace, the deadly
nightshade. In a clear sky Venus

is rising—Natural Venus and Celestial
Venus. There is a lamb in sheep's clothing
and a man in lamb's clothing. You arrived
by a dark path; but it was the only
path. You might dream of pausing
along the way and sleeping in a barn,
but only in the robes of a privy councillor.
Ancient neighborhoods and crumbling houses
with green shutters were gentrified
long after you passed through,
and now they gleam, new, unrecognizably.
In the equinoctial light of shipyards
and in the light of arctic shipyards,
you have stepped out onto the rose-patterned
stones of the common pathway.
And again, night comes, and the sky,
with all its stars, its boundlessness
coming to befriend you.

Summer Evening

People like to sit or walk along the promenade,
face the water and the setting sun under the tall
soft tree of summer evening when the breezes
grow cool and strong just prior to dusk. And the sun
dips down into the cool space behind the marina,
behind the dark green cliffs of summer evening,
like the plaything of a bygone era.
The blue and toy-like public vehicles reemerge,
reemerge and shine like glass before the substation.
The self seeks retribution; it seeks vindication—
we can let all of that rest for a moment. Let's watch
the youthful girls pass by, their bodies quince, seaspray,
ice plant, lichen. Under the trees, evening and summer
will come, and come to be known as living languages
that no one speaks, but everyone will understand.

To my fellow poets—Randall Potts, Tom King, David Joel Friedman, Molly Lou Freeman, Julien Marcland, Alex Cigale, Matthew Zapruder, Emily Wilson, Mark Levine— my deepest admiration and gratitude.

The bird a nest, the spider a web, man friendship. —Wm Blake